Just Stitches:

70 Knitting Stitch Patterns to Inspire Your Next Project

Abbreviation List:

K: knit

P: purl

St(s): stitch(es)

Sl: slip

YO: yarn over (yarn over needle)

Tog: together

K2tog: knit 2 stitches together

P2tog: purl 2 stitches together

PSSO: pass slipped stitch over

RS: right side

WS: wrong side

ISBN-13: 978-1496177551
ISBN-10: 149617755X

1. Garter Stitch

Cast on any number of sts

Knit across each row

2. Stockinette Stitch

Cast on any number of sts

Row 1: K across

Row 2: P across

Repeat rows 1 and 2 for pattern.

3. Basic Ribbing

Cast on a multiple of 4 sts plus 2

Row 1: K2, *P2, K2, repeat from * across row

Row 2: P2, *K2, P2, repeat from * across row

Repeat rows 1 and 2 for pattern

4. Craftsman Stitch

Cast on any number of sts

Row 1: K across row

Row 2: P across row

Row 3: K across row

Repeat rows 1-3 for pattern

5. Moss Stitch

Cast on any odd number of sts

Row 1: *K1, P1, repeat from * across row, ending with K1.

Repeat row 1 for pattern.

6. Chevron

Cast on a multiple of 8 sts plus 1

Row 1: *P1, K7, repeat from *, ending P1

Row 2: K2, *P5, K3, repeat from * across, ending K2.

Row 3: P3,* K3, P5, repeat from * across, ending P3.

Row 4: K4,* P1, K7, repeat from * across, ending K4.

Row 5: P across row.

Repeat rows 1-5 for pattern.

7. Back Stitch Stockinette

Cast on any number of sts

Row 1: K across row, knitting into back of stitch

Row 2: P across row

Repeat rows 1 and 2 for pattern

8. Double Rice Stitch

Cast on a multiple of 4 sts

Row 1: *K2, P2, repeat from * across row

Row 2: Repeat row 1

Row 3: *P2, K2, repeat from * across row

Row 4: Repeat row 3

Repeat rows 1-4 for pattern.

9. Sport Stitch

Cast on a multiple of 6 sts plus 2

Row 1: K3, P2, *K4, P2, repeat from * across row, ending K3

Row 2: P across row

Row 3: P2, *K4, P2, repeat from * across row

Row 4: P across row

Repeat rows 1-4 for pattern

10. Basket Weave Stitch

Cast on a multiple of 10 sts plus 3

Row 1: *K3, P7, repeat from * across row, ending with K3

Row 2: *P3, K7, repeat from * across row, ending P3

Row 3: repeat row 1

Row 4: P across row

Row 5: P5, *K3, P7, repeat from * across row, ending P5

Row 6: K5, *P3, K7, repeat from * across row, ending K5

Row 7: repeat row 5

Row 8: P across row

Repeat rows 1-8 for pattern

11. Vinay

Cast on a multiple of 13 sts

Row 1: *K2tog, K4, YO, K1, YO, K4, K2tog, repeat from * across row

Row 2: P across row

Repeat rows 1 and 2 for pattern

12. Open Striped Rows

Cast on a multiple of 8 sts plus 3

Row 1: *K3, K2tog, YO, K1, YO, K2tog, repeat from * across, ending K3

Row 2: P across row

Repeat rows 1 and 2 for pattern

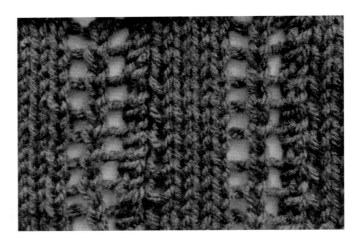

13. The Adair

Cast on a multiple of 16 sts

Row 1: K1, *(K2tog, YO) 3 times, K2, repeat from *, ending K1 instead of K2

Row 2: P across row

Row 3: repeat row 1

Row 4: repeat row 2

Row 5: K1, *K6, insert hook under and between the sts on left hook, pull up yarn, knit first st on needle, knit next st on needle, Pass pulled up st over 2 sts, repeat from * across, ending with K1

Repeat rows 1-5 for pattern

14. Block Rib Stitch

Cast on a multiple of 5 sts plus 3

Row 1: K across row

Row 2: P across row

Row 3: Repeat row 1

Row 4: Repeat row 2

Row 5: *K3, P2, repeat from * across row, ending K3

Row 6: *P3, K2, repeat from * across row, ending P3

Rows 7: Repeat row 5

Row 8: Repeat row 6

Repeat rows 1-8 for pattern

15. Broken Rib Stitch

Cast on a multiple of 7 sts plus 5

Row 1: *K5, P2, repeat from * across row, ending K5

Row 2: *P5, K2, repeat from * across row, ending P5

Repeat rows 1 and 2 for a total of 7 rows.

Row 8: K across row (this row forms a ridge on RS of work)

Repeat all 8 rows for pattern

16. Brick Repeat

Cast on a multiple of 4 sts

Row 1: *K2, YO, K2, slip YO over the 2 K sts, repeat from * across row

Row 2: P across row

Row 3: *YO, K2, slip YO over the 2 K sts, repeat from * across row

Row 4: P across row

Repeat rows 1-4 for pattern

17. Diagonal Rib Stitch

Cast on a multiple of 8 sts

Row 1: *K4, P4, repeat from * across row

Row 2 (WS): P1, *K4, P4, repeat from * across row, ending K4, P3

Row 3: K2, *P4, K4, repeat from * across row, ending P4, K2

Row 4: P3, *K4, P4, repeat from * across row, ending K4, P1

Row 5: *P4, K4, repeat from * across row

Row 6: K1, *P4, K4, repeat from * across row, ending P4, K3

Row 7: P2, *K4, P4, repeat from * across row, ending K4, P2

Row 8: K3, *P4, K4, repeat from * across row, ending P4, K1

Repeat rows 1-8 for pattern

18. Triangles

Cast on a multiple of 10 sts

Row 1: *K9, P1, repeat from * across row

Row 2: *K2, P8, repeat from * across row

Row 3: *K7, P3, repeat from * across row

Row 4: *K4, P6, repeat from * across row

Row 5: *K5, P5, repeat from * across row

Row 6: *K6, P4, repeat from * across row

Row 7: *K3, P7, repeat from * across row

Row 8: *K8, P2, repeat from * across row

Row 9: *K1, P9, repeat from * across row

Repeat row 9 and then reverse directions to and including row 1.

To repeat pattern, start over from row 1 again.

19. French Stitch

Cast on a multiple of 2 sts plus 1

Row 1: K1, *slip 1, K1, repeat from * across row

Row 2: P across row

Repeat rows 1 and 2 for pattern.

20. Square dot pattern

Cast on a multiple of 8 sts plus 1

Row 1: K1, P1, K5, *P1, K1, P1, K5, repeat from * across row, ending P1, K1.

Row 2: K1, *P7, K1, repeat from * across row

Row 3: K across row

Row 4: P4, K1, *P7, K1, repeat from * across row, ending P4

Row 5: K3, P1, K1, P1, *K5, P1, K1, P1, repeat from * across row, ending K3

Row 6: repeat row 4

Row 7: K across row

Row 8: repeat row 2

Repeat rows 1-8 for pattern

21. Herringbone

Cast on a multiple of 9 sts plus 1

Row 1: P across row

Row 2: *K2tog, K3, increase 1 st in next st (by K1 in back of next st in row below, then K the next st), K3, repeat from * across row, ending K4 instead of K3

Row 3: P across row

Row 4: K4, *increase 1 st in next st as in row 2, K3, K2tog, K3, repeat from * across row, ending increase 1 st in next st, K3, K2tog

Repeat rows 1-4 for pattern

22. All-Over Stitch

Cast on a multiple of 2 sts

Row 1: K across row

Row 2: P across row

Row 3: *K2 tog and before slipping them off left-hand needle, knit into the first st in usual manner, then slip both worked sts from left-hand needle (the 2 sts crossed in this way will, in future, be referred to as "C2sts"), repeat from * across row

Row 4: P across row

Row 5: K1, *C2sts, repeat from * across row, ending K1

Row 6: P across row

Repeat rows 1-6 for pattern

23. Popular Rib Stitch

Cast on a multiple of 4 sts

Row 1: *K1, P3, repeat from * across row

Row 2: P1, *K1, P3, repeat from * across row, ending P2

Repeat rows 1 and 2 for pattern

24. Double Loopy Loops

Cast on any number of sts

Row 1: K across row.

Row 2: insert right-hand needle through the loop of first st on left-hand needle, *pass the yarn over the points of both needles once and then around the point of right-hand needle only. Draw this last loop through the 2 loops on the left-hand needle and repeat from * across row.

Row 3: P across row

Row 4: P across row

Row 5: K across row

Row 6: P across row

Row 7: K across row

Repeat rows 2-7 for pattern

25. Odd Rib Stitch

Cast on an even number of sts

Row 1: *K1, P1, repeat from * across row

Rows 2 and 3: repeat row 1

Row 4: *P1, K1, repeat from * across row

Repeat rows 1-4 to make pattern

26. Cosmopolitan

Cast on a multiple of 4 sts

Row 1: *K3, P1, repeat from * across row

Row 2: K2, P1, *K3, P1, repeat from * across row, ending K1

Repeat rows 1 and 2 for pattern

27. Textured Dots

Cast on an even number of sts

Row 1: P across row

Row 2: K1, *K2, pick up the yarn below the st on the left needle and pull up a loop, K1 (the skipped st), pass the picked-up loop over the K1, repeat from * across row, ending K1

Row 3: P across row

Row 4: K1, *pick up the yarn below the st on the left needle and pull up a loop, K1 (the skipped st), pass the picked-up loop over the K1, K2, repeat from * across row, ending K1

Repeat rows 1-4 for pattern

28. Ribbed Border Stitch

Cast on a multiple of 3 sts plus 2

Row 1: P2, *increase 1 st in next st (by working K in front of st and K in back of st), P2, repeat from * across row

Row 2: K2, *P2tog, K2, repeat from * across row

Repeat rows 1 and 2 for pattern

29. Tweedsmuir

Cast on a multiple of 5 sts plus 2

Row 1: *P2, K2, slip 1 as if to P (yarn in back of work), repeat from * across row, ending P2

Row 2: *K2, yarn forward, slip 1, P2, repeat from * across row, ending K2

Row 3: *P2, (yarn in back of work), insert needle in slip st of previous row (3rd st on left hand needle), K it but do not slip it off needle, K first st on left hand needle and slip this st off needle, slip next st on to right hand needle, drop next st off needle (sl st of previous row), repeat from * across row, ending P2

Repeat rows 2 and 3 for pattern

30. Crossed Cardigan Stitch

Cast on a multiple of 3 sts plus 2

Row 1: K1, *YO, slip 1 as if to P, K2tog, repeat from * across row, ending K1

Repeat row 1 for pattern

31. Cayce

Cast on a multiple of 2 sts

Row 1: K1, *YO, slip 1 (as if to P), K1, repeat from * across row, ending K1

Row 2 (RS): K2, *K the YO and the slip st tog through back of sts, K1, repeat from * across row

Repeat rows 1 and 2 for pattern

32. Eyelet Mesh

Cast on any odd number of sts

Row 1: P across row

Row 2: K1, *YO, K2tog, repeat from * across row

Row 3: P across row

Row 4: K across row

Repeat rows 1-4 for pattern

33. Open Work Squares

Cast on a multiple of 8 sts plus 3 sts

Row 1: K1, *YO, slip 1, K1, PSSO, repeat from * across row

Row 2: P across row

Row 3: K3, *YO, slip 1, K1, PSSO, K6, repeat from * across row

Row 4: P across row

Repeat rows 3 and 4, 3 more times

Repeat all 10 rows for pattern

34. Diagonal Eyelet Stitch

Cast on a multiple of 4 sts

Row 1: *P2, P2tog, YO, repeat from * across row, ending P4

Row 2: K across row

Row 3: P across row

Row 4: K across row

Row 5: P4, *P2tog, YO, P2, repeat from * across row

Row 6: K across row

Row 7: P across row

Row 8: K across row

Repeat rows 1-8 for pattern

35. Tear Drop

Cast on a multiple of 4 sts plus 1

Row 1: P1, *work 5 sts in next st (K1, P1, K1, P1, K1), P3, repeat from * across row

Row 2: *K3, P5, repeat from * across row, ending K1

Row 3: P1, *K5, P3, repeat from * across row

Row 4: repeat row 2

Row 5: P1, *slip 1 as if to K, K1, PSSO, K1, K2tog, P3, repeat from * across row

Row 6: K3, P3, repeat from * across row, ending K1

Row 7: *P1, slip 1, K2tog, PSSO, P1, work 5 sts in next st as in row 1, repeat from * across row, ending P1

Row 8: K1, *P5, K3, repeat from * across row

Row 9: *P3, K5, repeat from * across row, ending P1

Row 10: K1, *P5, K3, repeat from * across row

Row 11: *P3, slip 1, K1, PSSO, K1, K2tog, repeat from * across row, ending P1

Row 12: K1, *P3, K3, repeat from * across row

Row 13: *P1, work 5 sts in next st, P1, slip 1, K2tog, PSSO, repeat from * across row, ending P1

Repeat rows 2-13 for pattern

36. English Lace Pattern

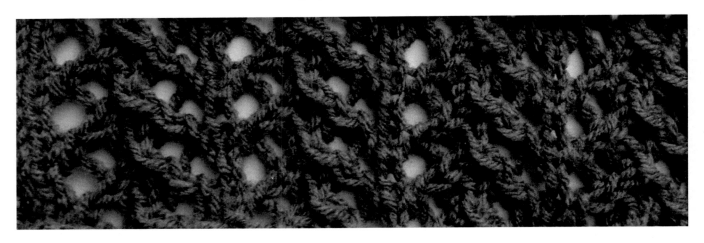

Cast on a multiple of 6 sts plus 4

Row 1: K2, *YO, slip 1, K1, PSSO, K1, K2tog, YO, K1, repeat from * across row, ending K2

Row 2: P across row

Row 3: K3, *YO, slip 1, K2tog, PSSO, YO, K3, repeat from * across row, ending K1

Row 4: P across row

Repeat rows 1-4 for pattern

37. Blackberry Stitch

Cast on a multiple of 4 sts plus 1

Row 1 (RS): P across row

Row 2: (K1, P1, K1) all in the same st, *P3tog, (K1, P1, K1) in the next st, repeat from * across row, ending (K1, P1, K1) in last st

Row 3: P across row

Row 4: *P3tog, (K1, P1, K1) in the next st, repeat from * across row, ending P3tog

Repeat rows 1-4 for pattern

38. The Carson

Cast on a multiple of 4 sts plus 2

Row 1: P across row

Row 2: *K2, pick up the yarn below the 2 next sts on the left needle and pull up a loop, K2 (slipping st off hook after each K), pass the picked-up loop over the K2, repeat from * across row, ending K2

Repeat rows 1 and 2 for pattern

39. Fancy Turkish Stitch

Cast on a multiple of 3 sts

Row 1: *P1, K the second st on the left-hand needle, leave the st on needle and K the first st, slip off both sts and repeat from * across row

Row 2: *K1, P the second st on the left-hand needle, leave on the needle, P the first st, slip off both sts and repeat from * across row

Repeat rows 1 and 2 for pattern

40. Plaza

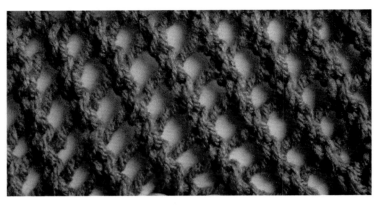

Cast on an even number of sts

Row 1: K1, *YO, K2tog, repeat from * across row, ending K1

Row 2: P across row

Row 3: K2, *YO, K2tog, repeat from * across row

Row 4: P across row

Row 5: K1, *K2tog, YO, repeat from * across row, ending YO, K1

Row 6: P across row

Repeat rows 1-6 for pattern

41. Open Dot Stitch

Cast on a multiple of 8 sts, plus 1

Row 1: P1, *K7, P1, repeat from * across row

Row 2: K1, *P7, K1, repeat from * across row

Row 3: repeat row 1

Row 4: repeat row 2

Row 5: P1, *K2, YO, slip 1, K2tog, PSSO, YO, K2, P1, repeat from * across row

Row 6: repeat row 2

Row 7: repeat row 5

Row 8: repeat row 2

Repeat rows 1-8 for pattern

42. Rosebud Pattern

Cast on a multiple of 6 sts

Row 1: P5, *K1, YO, P5, repeat from * across row, ending YO, P5

Row 2: *K5, P2, repeat from * across row, ending K5

Row 3: *P5, K2, repeat from * across row, ending P5

Row 4: *K5, P2, repeat from * across row, ending K5

Row 5: repeat row 3

Row 6: *K5, P2tog, repeat from * across row, ending K5

Row 7: P2, *K1, YO, P5, repeat from * across row, ending YO, P2

Row 8: K2, *P2, K5, repeat from * across row, ending K2

Row 9: P2, *K2, P5, repeat from * across row, ending P2

Row 10: repeat row 8

Row 11: repeat row 9

Row 12: K2, *P2tog, K5, repeat from * across row, ending P2tog, K2

Repeat rows 1-12 for pattern

43. Turkish Stitch

Cast on an odd number of sts

Row 1: K1, * YO, K2tog, repeat from * across row

Repeat row 1 for pattern

44. Open Hole Stripes

Cast on a multiple of 8 sts

Row 1: *P4, K2tog, YO, K2, repeat from * across row

Row 2: *P2tog, YO, P2, K4, repeat from * across row

Repeat rows 1 and 2 for pattern

45. Dots and Stripes

Cast on a multiple of 6 sts plus 1.

Row 1: K1, *P5, K1, repeat from * across row

Row 2: P1, *K5, P1, repeat from * across row

Row 3: K1, *P2, (K1, P1, K1, P1, K1) all in the next st, P2, K1, repeat from * across row

Row 4: P1, *K9, P1, repeat from * across row

Row 5: K1, *P2, P5tog, P2, K1, repeat from * across row

Row 6: Repeat row 2

Repeat rows 1-6 for pattern.

46. Open Work Stripes

Cast on a multiple of 7sts plus 4

Row 1: K4, *YO, slip 1, K2tog, PSSO, YO, K4, repeat from * across row

Row 2: K1, P to last st, K1

Row 3: K across row

Row 4: repeat row 2

Repeat rows 1-4 for pattern

47. Joplin

Cast on a multiple of 16 sts

Row 1: *K2, P2, repeat from * across row

Rows 2 and 3: same as row 1

Row 4: *insert needle between 6th and 7th st, YO needle, pull up a loop, then K the first st, P2tog, P1, K2, P2, repeat from * across row

Rows 5, 6, and 7: same as row 1

Row 8: K2, P2, repeat from * of row 4 across row, ending K2, P2

Repeat rows 1-8 for pattern

48. Twisted Stitches #1

Cast on a multiple of 4 sts plus 2.

Row 1: *K2, twist 2 (by sk 1 st, K the next st through back loop in back of work, then K the skipped st), repeat from * across row, ending K2.

Row 2: P across row

Row 3: repeat row 1

Row 4: P across row

Row 5: *twist 2 (as in Row 1), K2, repeat from * across row, ending twist 2.

Row 6: P across row

Repeat rows 1-6 for pattern.

49. Twisted Stitches #2

Cast on a multiple of 4 sts plus 2.

Row 1: *K2, twist 2 (by sk 1 st, K the next st through back loop in back of work, then K the skipped st), repeat from * across row, ending K2.

Row 2: *P2, *twist 2 (sk 1 st, P next st in front of work, then P the skipped st), repeat from * across row, ending P2.

Repeat rows 1 and 2 for pattern.

50. Twisted Stitches #3

Cast on a multiple of 4 sts plus 2.

Row 1: *K2, twist 2 (by sk 1 st, K the next st through back loop in back of work, then K the skipped st), repeat from * across row, ending K2.

Row 2: *twist 2 (sk 1 st, P next st in front of work, then P the skipped st), P2, repeat from * across row, ending twist 2.

Repeat rows 1 and 2 for pattern.

51. Twisted Stitches #4

Cast on a multiple of 4 sts plus 2.

Row 1: *K2, twist 2 (by sk 1 st, K the next st through back loop in back of work, then K the skipped st), repeat from * across row, ending K2.

Row 2: P across row

Row 3: repeat row 1

Row 4: P1, *twist 2 (by sk 1 st, K the next st through back loop in back of work, then P the skipped st), twist 2 (sk 1 st, P next st in front of work, then P the skipped st), repeat from * across row, ending P1.

Row 5: *twist 2 (as in Row 1), K2, repeat from * across row, ending twist 2.

Row 6: P across row

Row 7: repeat row 5

Row 8: P1, *twist 2 (sk 1 st, P next st in front of work, then P the skipped st), twist next 2 (by sk 1 st, K the next st through back loop in back of work, then P the skipped st), repeat from * across row, ending P1.

Repeat rows 1-8 for pattern.

52. Lacy Wave

Cast on a multiple of 10 sts plus 1

Row 1: K1, *YO, K2tog, K5, K2tog, YO, K1, repeat from * across row, ending YO, K1

Row 2: P across row

Row 3: K2, *YO, K2tog, K3, K2tog, YO, K3, repeat from * across row, ending YO, K2

Row 4: P across row

Row 5: K3, *YO, K2tog, K1, K2tog, YO, K5, repeat from * across row, ending YO, K3

Row 6: P across row

Row 7: K4, *YO, slip 1, K2tog, PSSO, YO, K7, repeat from * across row, ending YO, K4

Row 8: P across row

Repeat rows 1-8 for pattern

53. Rib Lace Stitch

Cast on a multiple of 5 sts plus 2

Row 1: *K2, P3tog, repeat from * across row, ending K2

Row 2: *P2, YO, P1, YO, repeat from * across row, ending P2

Repeat rows 1 and 2 for pattern

54. Wheat Ear Pattern

Cast on a multiple of 7sts plus 4

Row 1: K2, *K1, YO, slip 1, K1, PSSO, K2tog, K2, YO, repeat from * across row, ending YO, K2

Row 2: P across row

Row 3: K2, *YO, slip 1, K1, PSSO, K2tog, K2, YO, K1, repeat from * across row, ending K2

Row 4: P across row

Repeat rows 1-4 for pattern

55. Cablette

Cast on a multiple of 5 sts plus 2

Row 1: *P2, K3, repeat from * across row, ending P2

Row 2: *K2, P3, repeat from * across row, ending K2

Row 3: *P2, slip 1, K2, PSSO the 2 K sts, repeat from * across row, ending P2

Row 4: *K2, P1, YO, P1, repeat from * across row, ending K2

Repeat rows 1-4 for pattern

56. *Duchess*

Cast on a multiple of 10 sts plus 5

Row 1: K2, slip 1, K1, PSSO, *K4, YO, K1, YO, K2, slip 1, K2tog, PSSO, repeat from * across row, ending row (last 4 sts) slip 1, K1, PSSO, K2

Row 2 and all even rows: P across row

Row 3: K2, slip 1, K1, PSSO, *K3, YO, K3, YO, K1, slip 1, K2tog, PSSO, repeat from * across row, ending row slip 1, K1, PSSO, K2

Row 5: K2, slip 1, K1, PSSO, *K2, YO, K5, slip 1, K2tog, PSSO, repeat from * across row, ending row slip 1, K1, PSSO, K2. From the 5th to the 10th row inclusive there will be 9sts in each pattern but on row 11 the original number of 10 sts will be regained.

Row 7: K2, slip 1, K1, PSSO, *K1, YO, K1, YO, K4, slip 1, K2tog, PSSO, repeat from * across row, ending row slip 1, K1, PSSO, K2

Row 9: K2, slip 1, K1, PSSO, *YO, K3, YO, K3, slip 1, K2tog, PSSO, repeat from * across row, ending row slip 1, K1, PSSO, K2

Row 11: K1, slip 1, K1, PSSO, *YO, K5, YO, K2, slip 1, K1, PSSO, repeat from * across row, ending row YO, K last 6 sts

Row 12: P across row

Repeat rows 1-12 for pattern

57. Diamond Repeat

Cast on a multiple of 6 sts plus 1

Row 1: K2, *YO, K2tog, K1, YO, slip 1, K1, PSSO, K1, repeat from * across row, ending YO, K2tog

Row 2 and all even rows: P across row

Row 3: K3, *K2tog, YO, K1, YO, slip 1, K1, PSSO, K1, repeat from * across row, ending K2

Row 5: K1, *YO, slip 1, K2tog, PSSO, YO, K3, repeat from * across row, ending YO, K2tog, K1

Row 7: K2, *YO, slip 1, K1, PSSO, K1, YO, K2tog, K1, repeat from * across row, ending YO, slip 1, K1, PSSO

Row 9: *K2tog, YO, K1, YO, slip 1, K1, PSSO, K1, repeat from * across row, ending K2tog, YO, K2

Row 11: K4, *YO, slip 1, K2tog, PSSO, YO, K3, repeat from * across row

Row 12: P across row

Repeat rows 1-12 for pattern

58. Sidewinder

Cast on a multiple of 6 sts

Row 1: K across row

Row 2: K, wrapping yarn around needle twice in each st

Row 3: *slip first 6 sts, dropping extra loop as you do. With point of left hand needle slip first 3 sts over 2nd 3 sts and off needle, slip the remaining 3 sts back on to left hand needle and K increasing 1 st in each st (increase by K in front and back of st), repeat from * across row

Row 4: K across row

Repeat rows 1-4 for pattern

59. Enli

Cast on a multiple of 4 sts plus 2

Row 1: K across row

Row 2: *K2, YO, slip 1, YO, slip 1, repeat from * across row, ending K2

Row 3: *P2, K the slip st and the YO above it tog through back (twisting the st), K the next sl st and YO tog as before, repeat from * across row, ending P2

Repeat rows 1-3 for pattern

60. Cross Stitch Mesh

Cast on a multiple of 3 sts

Row 1: K2, *YO, K3, pass first K st over 2 K sts, repeat from * across row, ending K1

Row 2: P across row

Row 3: K1, *YO, K3, pass first K st over 2 K sts, repeat from * across row, ending K2

Row 4: P across row

Repeat rows 1-4 for pattern

61. Tamerna

Cast on a multiple of 5 sts

Row 1: *K1, P1, K2, P1, repeat from * across row

Row 2: *K1, P2, K1, P1, repeat from * across row

Row 3: *K1, P1, knit in back of 2nd st on left hand needle, but leave it on the needle, knit the first st on needle, take off both sts, P1, repeat from * across row

Row 4: repeat row 2

Repeat rows 1-4 for pattern

62. Cable Rib Stitch

Cast on a multiple of 9 sts plus 2

Row 1: K2, *P2, K3, P2, K2, repeat from * across row

Row 2: P2, *K2, P3, K2, P2, repeat from * across row

Row 3: K2, *P2, K3tog, and before taking these 3 sts off left hand needle, purl into them, then knit into them, thus replacing the stitches knitted together, P2, K2, repeat from * across row

Row 4: repeat row 2

Repeat rows 1-4 for pattern

63. Marquise

Cast on a multiple of 8 sts

Row 1: *K1, YO, K2, slip 1, K2tog, PSSO, K2, YO, repeat from *, ending K 2 sts in last st (instead of YO)

Row 2: P across row

Row 3: *K2, YO, K1, slip 1, K2tog, PSSO, K1, YO, K1, repeat from * across row

Row 4: P across row

Row 5: *K3, YO, slip 1, K2tog, PSSO, YO, K2, repeat from * across row

Row 6: P across row

Repeat rows 1-6 for pattern

64. Camulo

Cast on a multiple of 9 sts plus 3

Row 1: P3, *YO, K3, slip the YO over the 3 sts, K3, P3, repeat from * across row

Rows 2, 4, 6, and 8: K3, *P6, K3, repeat from * across row

Row 3: P3, *K1, YO, K3, slip the YO over the 3 sts, K2, P3, repeat from * across row

Row 5: P3, *K2, YO, K3, slip the YO over the 3 sts, K1, P3, repeat from * across row

Row 7: P3, *K3, YO, K3, slip the YO over the 3 sts, P3, repeat from * across row

Repeat rows 1-8 for pattern

65. Pointed Stripe

Row 1: K2tog, K2, *YO, K1, YO, K2, slip 1, K1, PSSO, K2tog K2, repeat from * across row

Row 2: P across row

Repeat rows 1 and 2 for pattern

Cast on a multiple of 9 sts

66. Rib and Cable Stripes

Cast on a multiple of 6 sts plus 2

Row 1: *P2, K4, repeat from * across row, ending P2

Row 2: *K2, P4, repeat from * across row, ending K2

Row 3: P2, *(skip next st but do not slip from needle, K1 in the next st, K the missed st and slip both off needle tog) 2 times, P2, repeat from * across row

Row 4: repeat row 2

Row 5: repeat row 1

Row 6: repeat row 2

Row 7: P2, * (with needle in back of work K into back of second st, K into front of first st, slip both off needle tog) 2 times, P2, repeat from * across row

Row 8: repeat row 2

Repeat rows 1-8 for pattern

67. Triple Cross Stitch Band

Cast on 21 sts

Row 1: K4, YO, slip 1, K2tog, PSSO, YO, P2, YO, slip 1, K2tog, PSSO, YO, P2, YO, slip 1, K2tog, PSSO YO, K4

Row 2: P7, K2, P3, K2, P7

Row 3: K7, *P2, K3, P2, K7

Row 4: repeat row 2

Repeat rows 1-4 for pattern

68. Feather and Fan with Rib

Cast on a multiple of 18 sts

Row 1: (K2tog 3 times), *K1 and YO 6 times), (K2tog 6 times), repeat from * across row, ending with (K2tog 3 times)

Row 2: P across row

Row 3: K across row

Row 4: K across row

Repeat rows 1-4 for pattern.

69. Knob Stitch

Cast on a multiple of 20 sts plus 1

Row 1: K1, *P9, K1, repeat from * across row.

Row 2 and all even rows: P1, *K9, P1, repeat from * across row.

Row 3: K1, *P4, work (K1, P1, K1, P1, K1, P1) all in the next st then take 5 sts off by slipping 1 st over the other until one st remains (forming 1 knob st), P4, K1, P9, K1, repeat from * across row.

Row 5: K1, *P3, work 1 knob in next st, P1, work 1 knob in next st, P3, K1, P9, repeat from * across row.

Row 7: repeat row 3

Row 9: K1, *P9, K1, P4, 1 knob in next st, P4, K1, repeat from * across row.

Row 11: K1, *P9, K1, P3, 1 knob in next st, P1, 1 knob in next st, P3, K1, repeat from * across row.

Row 13: repeat row 9

Row 14: repeat row 2

Repeat rows 3-14 for pattern.

70. Leaf design

Cast on a multiple of 10 sts plus 3

Row 1: K5, *YO, slip 1, K2tog, PSSO, YO, K7, repeat from * across row, ending K5 instead of K7

Row 2 and all even rows: P across row

Row 3: K2tog, K3, *YO, K3, YO, K2, slip 1, K2tog, PSSO, K2, repeat from * across row, ending YO, K3, YO, K3, K2tog

Row 5: K2tog, K2, *YO, K5, YO, K1, slip 1, K2tog, PSSO, K1, repeat from * across row, ending YO, K5, YO, K2, K2tog

Row 7: K2tog, K1, *YO, K7, YO, slip 1, K2tog, PSSO, repeat from * across row, ending YO, K7, YO, K1, K2tog

Row 9: K3, *YO, K2, slip 1, K2tog, PSSO, K2, YO, K3, repeat from * across row

Row 11: K4, *YO, K1, slip 1, K2tog, PSSO, K1, YO, K5, repeat from * across row, ending K4 instead of K5

Row 12: P across row

Repeat rows 1-12 for pattern

35061933R00022

Made in the USA
Middletown, DE
01 February 2019